I0408896

ADOBE AFTER EFFECTS GUIDEBOOK

The Comprehensive Guide with Illustrations to master After Effects

By

Kai Torres

Copyright ©2023 Kai Torres

All rights reserved

Table of Contents

CHAPTER 1: GETTING TO KNOW THE WORKFLOW

Creating a Project and Importing Footage

1. After launching After Effects, hold down Ctrl+Alt+Shift (Windows) or Command+Option+Shift (MacOS) to return to the program's default preferences. Click OK to remove your choices when prompted.

   Home window appears. It offers quick access to tutorials and additional After Effects knowledge, as well as your most recent After Effects work.

2. Inside the Home window, select New Project.

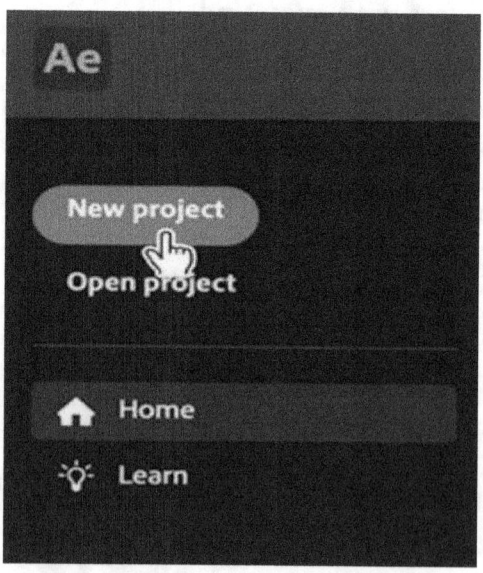

Each piece of video you utilize in an After Effects project is referenced in a single file called the project. Compositions, which are discrete containers used to integrate footage, apply effects, and ultimately control the result, are also included in it.

It seems like you're following instructions for importing files and saving a project in Adobe After Effects. Here's a breakdown of the steps you provided:

3. Choose File > Import > File.

4. Go to your Lessons/Lesson01 folder and choose the Assets folder. Select the files movement.mp3 and swimming_dog.mp4 by holding down the Shift key. Click Import or Open after that.

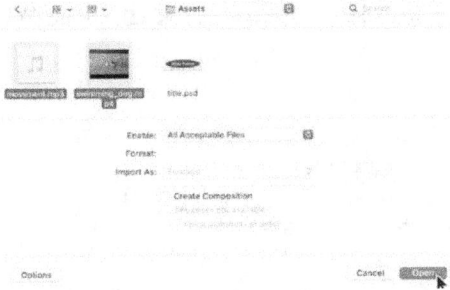

5. To bring up the Import File dialog box, double-click in the lower portion of the Project panel.

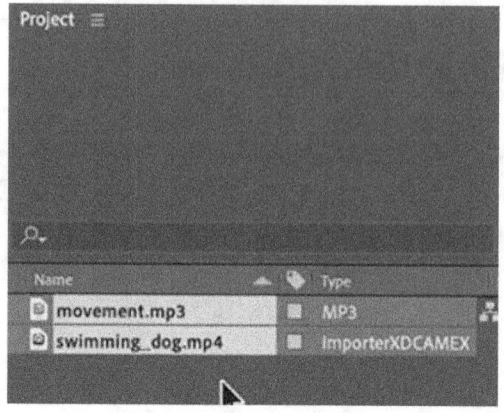

6. Return to Lesson01/Assets and choose the title.psd file this time. Composition can be selected from the Import As menu. You might need to click Options in macOS to get the Import As menu. Click Import or Open after that.

The parameters for the file you are importing are displayed in a separate dialog box that After Effects opens.

7. To import the layered Photoshop file as a composition, select Composition from the Import Kind menu in the title.psd dialog box. Click OK after selecting Editable Layer Styles in the Layer Options section.

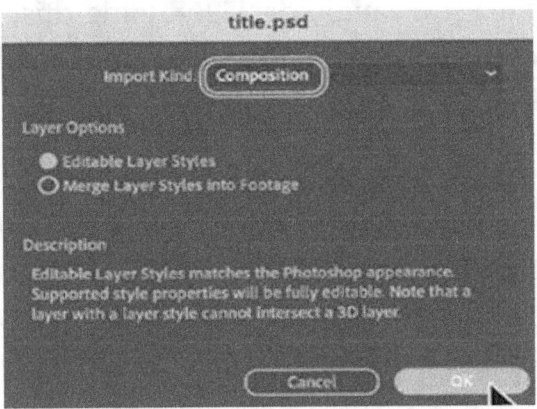

8. Click on several footage items in the Project tab to choose them. At the top of the Project panel, you'll see a thumbnail preview. In the Project panel columns, you can also view the file type, size, and other details for each item.

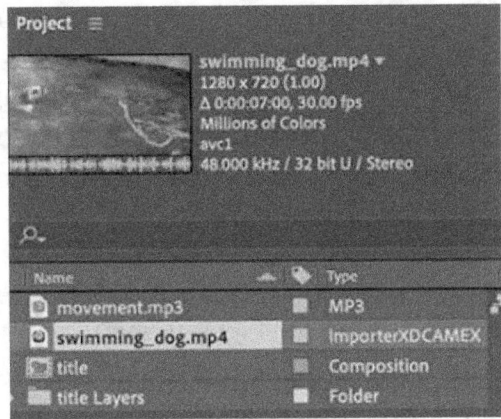

After Effects doesn't replicate the video and audio data into your project when you import files. Instead, a reference link to the source files is included with each item of footage in the Project panel. After Effects reads the source file when it wants to access image or audio data. By doing this, you can update source files in another application without having to change the project file size.

After Effects will notify you that a file is missing if you relocate it or if it can't access its location. Select File > Dependencies > Find Missing Footage to locate missing files. To search for the missing assets, you may also type Missing Footage into the Project panel's Search box.

Even if a film item is used numerous times in a composition, you often only import it once to save time and reduce the size and complexity of a project. To use a source file at two distinct frame rates, for example, you might occasionally need to import it more than once.

It's a good idea to save the project after importing the video.

9. Selecting File > Save. Navigate to the Lessons/Lesson01/Finished_Project folder in the Save As dialog box. Click Save after naming the project Lesson01_Finished.aep.

Creating a Composition and Arranging Layers

The workflow then moves on to phase two, composition creation. In a composition, you generate all of the animation, layering, and effects. The spatial and temporal elements of an After Effects composition are both time.

Layers are arranged in the Timeline panel and Composition panel of compositions, which may contain one or more layers. A composition gains a new layer whenever you add something to it, whether a still image, a moving image, an audio file, a light layer, a camera layer, or even another composition. One composition may be used in simple projects while multiple compositions may be used in elaborate projects to organize substantial quantities of video or complex effects sequences.

Drag the footage pieces into the Timeline window to start composing. After Effects will then build layers for the footage objects.

1. Shift-click the movement.mp3, swimming_dog.mp4, and title assets in the Project panel to choose them. Choose not to open the Layers folder.

2. The Timeline tab should now contain the selected footage elements. The dialog window for New Composition From Selection displays.

    A piece of video becomes the source for a new layer when it is added to a composition. A composition may contain any number of layers, and nesting is the process of including one composition as a layer in another.

3. Even though certain assets are longer than others, you only want them to continue while the swimming dog is

visible on the screen. To match the dog clip, you'll adjust the composition's overall duration to 7:00.

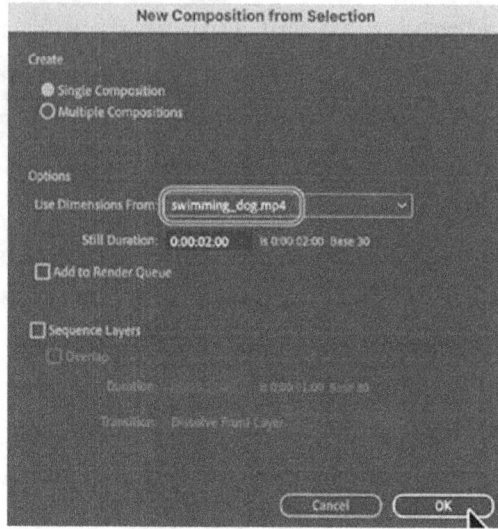

4. Select Settings > Composition from the menu.

5. Change the composition movement's name, enter 7:00 for the Duration, and click OK in the Composition Settings dialog box.

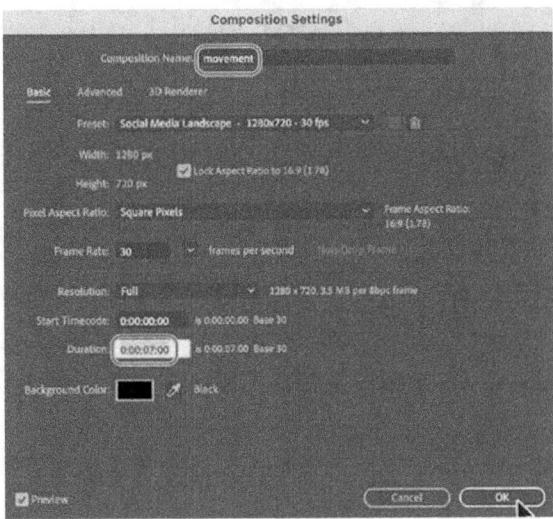

Each layer's duration in the Timeline panel is the same.

There are three footage elements in this composition, and the Timeline panel displays three layers as a result. Your layer stack might not be exactly the same as the one displayed on the previous page depending on the order in which the elements were chosen when you imported them. However, as you add effects and animations, the layers must be in a precise order, therefore you will reorganize them presently.

6. If the title layer is not already at the top of the layer stack, drag it there by clicking an empty space in the Timeline panel to deselect the layers. Move the layer containing movement.mp3 to the bottom of the layer stack.

7. To save your project thus far, select File > Save.

Adding Effects and Modifying Layer Properties

You may now have fun applying effects, creating transformations, and including motion once your composition is put up. Any effects can be combined, and any layer's attributes, including size, position, and opacity, can be changed. With the use of effects, you can change the look or sound of a layer or even create entirely new visual components. Applying one of the many After Effects' hundreds of effects is the simplest way to get started.

Changing Transform properties

The dog is currently hidden and the action is being distracted by the title, which is currently in the middle of the screen. It will be visible but out of the way if you relocate it to the lower left corner.

1. In the Timeline panel, choose the title layer (layer 1). In the Composition panel, you'll see that layer handles surround the layer.

2. Expand the layer by clicking the arrow to the left of the layer number, and then expand the Transform properties for the layer, which include Anchor Point, Position, Scale, Rotation, and Opacity.

3. Use the scroll bar on the Timeline panel's right side to go down the panel if you can't see the properties. Even better, choose the title layer name once more.

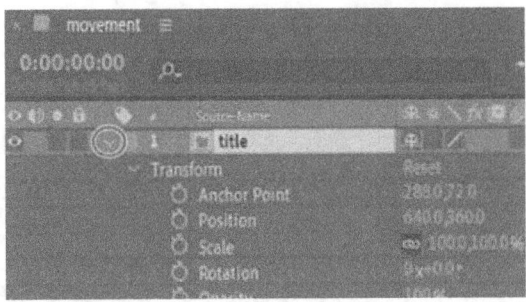

Then, hit P.

4. Set the Position property's coordinates to 265 and 635. Alternatively, you can drag the title to the screen's lower left corner using the Selection tool.

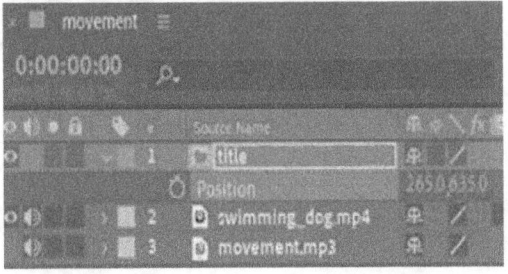

5. To conceal all properties, click the arrow to the left of the layer number, or press P to reveal the Position property.

Adding an effect to correct color

Several effects are available in After Effects to adjust or change the color of your projects. The Auto Contrast effect will be used to enhance the water's color and change the clip's overall contrast.

1. In the Timeline panel, choose the layer named swimming_dog.mp4.

2. To search for contrast, open the Effects & Presets panel by clicking on it in the panel stack on the right side of the program window.

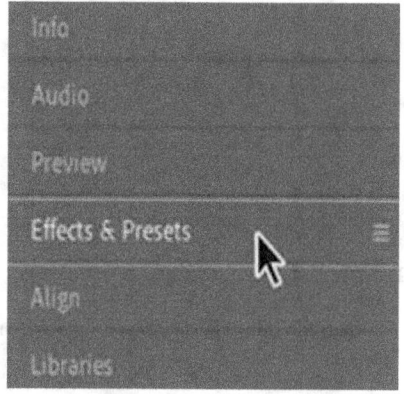

Then, input Contrast in the search bar.

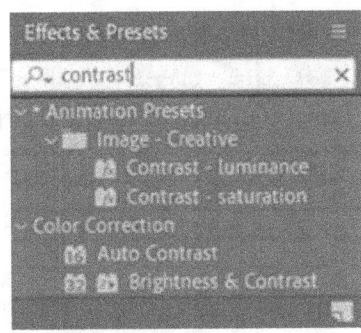

3. On the swimming_dog layer in the Timeline panel, drag the Auto Contrast effect.

   Colors are slightly overemphasized by the contrast. To lessen the effect, you'll adjust the settings.

4. Click the number next to Blend With Original in the Effect Controls window, enter 20% there, and then hit Enter or Return to accept the adjustment.

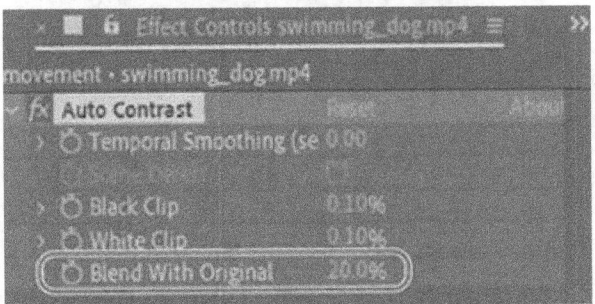

Animating the Composition

Using traditional keyframing, expressions, or keyframe helpers, you can alter any combination of a layer's characteristics over time in After Effects. Many of these techniques will be covered in this book's lessons. In order to introduce the title to the screen for this project, you'll use an animation preset, and you'll animate the title's color over time.

Preparing the text composition

You'll use a different composition for this.

1. Double-click the title composition to open it as a separate composition in its own Timeline panel after selecting the Project tab to show the Project panel.

In the Timeline panel, there are two layers: Ellipse 1 and Title Here. Photoshop-made placeholder text can be found on the Title Here layer.

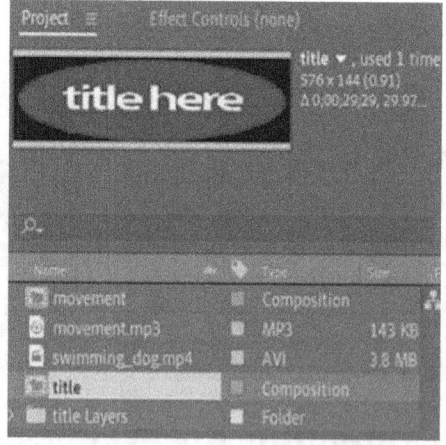

The Composition Navigator bar, which is located at the top of the Composition panel, shows the connection between the main composition (movement) and the present composition (title), which is nested within the main composition.

You can nest multiple compositions within each other; the Composition Navigator bar displays the entire composition path. Arrows between the composition names indicate the direction in which information flows.

Before you can replace the text, you need to make the layer editable.

    2. Select the Title Here layer (layer 1) in the Timeline panel, and then choose Layer > Create > Convert To Editable Text.

A T icon appears next to the layer name in the Timeline panel, indicating that it is now an editable text layer. The layer is also selected in the Composition panel, ready for you to edit.

The blue lines at the top, bottom, and sides of the Composition panel indicate title-safe and action-safe zones. Television sets enlarge a video image and allow some portion of its outer edges to be cut off by the edge of the screen. This is known as overscan. The amount of overscan is not consistent between television sets, so you should keep important parts of a video image, such as action or titles, within margins called safe zones. Keep your text inside the inner blue guides to ensure that it is in the title-safe zone, and keep important scene elements inside the outer blue guides to ensure that they are in the action-safe zone.

Editing Text

1. To pick the placeholder text in the Composition panel, choose the Horizontal Type tool (T) from the Tools panel. Next, type while moving.

2. Select the text again. Then, in the Character panel (docked on the right side of the screen), change the text size to 100 px and the tracking to −50.

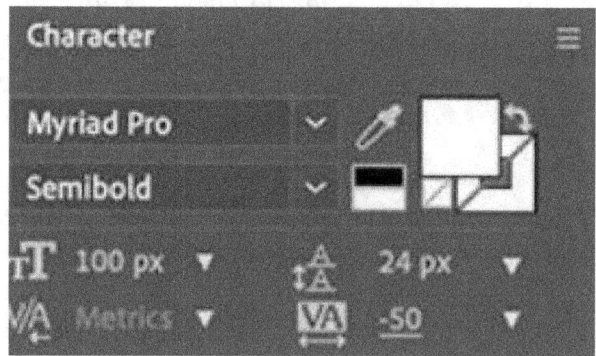

Animating effects using keyframes

The type layer will receive an effect, but this time you'll animate its settings via keyframes.

1. Do one of the following to return to the time ruler's beginning:

To position the current time indicator at 0:00, move it to the left on the time ruler.

In the Timeline panel or Composition panel, click the Current Time area and enter 00. Click OK to close the Go To Time dialog box if you selected the Current Time field in the Composition panel.

2. Enter "channel blur" in the Effects & Presets panel's search field.

3. On the Title Here layer in the Timeline panel, drag the Channel Blur effect.

The Channel Blur effect is added to the layer by After Effects, and the Effect Controls panel shows its parameters. Red, green, blue, and alpha channels of a layer are all separately blurred by the Channel Blur effect. It will give the title a unique appearance.

4. Set the Red Blurriness, Green Blurriness, Blue Blurriness, and Alpha Blurriness values to 50 in the Effect Controls panel.

5. To create the first keyframes, click the stopwatch icon (Stopwatch icon) next to each option you modified. The initial appearance of the words will be hazy.

Animation, effects, audio attributes, and many other types of changes that take place over time are created and controlled using keyframes. When you define a value, such as spatial position, opacity, or audio volume, you designate it with a keyframe. Values are interpolated in between keyframes. Use at least two keyframes—one for the state at the start of the change and one for the state at the end of the change—when using keyframes to make changes over time.

6. Select Vertical from the Blur Dimensions menu.

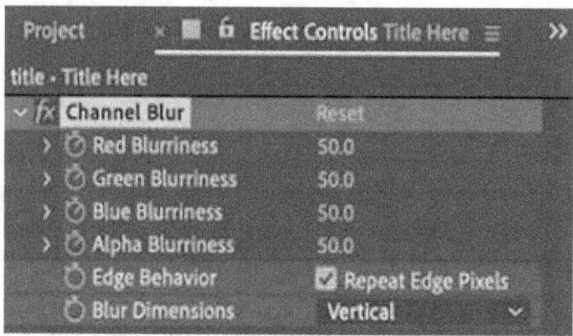

7. Go to 1:00 in the timeline.

8. Change the values to the following:

- Red Blurriness: 0

- Green Blurriness: 0

- Blue Blurriness: 0

- Alpha Blurriness: 0

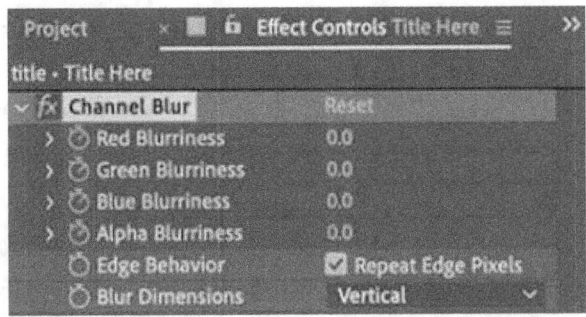

9. By manually advancing the current-time indication from 0 to 1:00, you can preview the effect.

Changing the opacity of the background

The ellipse is too bright, but the title looks fine. You'll adjust its opacity to let you see the water in the movie.

1. Select the Ellipse 1 layer in the Timeline panel.

2. To view the layer's Opacity attribute, press T.

3. 20% is the new number for opacity.

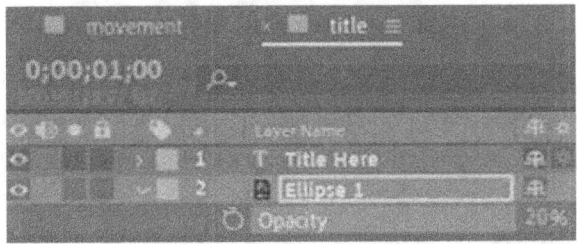

Optimizing Performance in After Effects

Depending on how After Effects and your machine are configured, After Effects can generate projects quickly. Complex compositions might require a lot of memory to render, and storing the resulting movies can take up a lot of disk space. Search for "Improve Performance" in the After Effects Help area to find tips on how to set up your system, After Effects preferences, and your projects for better performance.

After Effects by default enables GPU acceleration for effects, layer animations, and other features that may profit from the performance improvements. Adobe recommends activating GPU acceleration. If an error occurs or you are aware that the GPU in your system is incompatible with After Effects, you can disable GPU acceleration for the project: By choosing File > Project Settings, select Mercury Software Only from the Video Rendering And Effects menu.

Customizing Workspaces

You might have opened new panels or changed the size or positioning of some during the course of this project. When you make changes to a workspace, After Effects stores those changes so that the most recent workspace version is used when you start the project again. However, you always have the option to reset "Default" to saved layout by selecting Window > Workspace > Reset "Default" To Saved Layout.

Alternatively, you can save time by tailoring the workspace to your needs if you frequently use panels that aren't included in the Default workspace or if you want to resize or group panels for various types of projects. You can use any of the pre-configured workspaces that come with After Effects or save any workspace configuration. These pre-designed workspaces are appropriate for a variety of workflows, including work on animation or effects.

The panels that you would typically utilize for animation tasks, such as Motion Sketch, Wiggler, and Smoother, open in After Effects.

- Using the Workspace menu, you can switch workplaces as well.

- Choose Motion Tracking under Window > Workspace.

- Various panes open. You have quick access to tools and controls that are frequently used when monitoring motion in the Info, Preview, Tracker, and Content-Aware Fill panels.

Saving a custom workspace

Any workspace, at any time, can be saved as a custom workspace. When a workspace is saved, it is added to the Workspace bar at the top of the program window and the Window > Workspace submenu. After Effects searches for a workspace with a similar name when a project with a custom workspace is opened on a different system than the one it was made on. After Effects starts the project using the current local workspace if it can find a match (and the monitor configuration matches). If it can't find a match (or the monitor configuration doesn't match), it uses the workspace that is currently selected by the user.

1. By selecting Close Panel from its panel menu, you can close a panel.

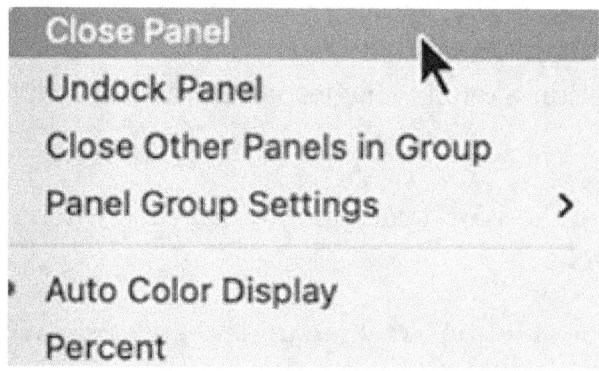

2. Another panel can be opened by selecting Window > Effects & Presets.

   The Effects & Presets panel is added to the panel stack.

3. Then select Save As New Workspace under Window > Workspace. Give the workspace a name, then click OK to save it. If you don't want to save it, click Cancel.

4. To bring back the original panels, select Default in the Workspace bar.

Controlling the brightness of the user interface

The user interface for After Effects can be either lighter or darker. Panels, windows, and dialog boxes are all affected when the brightness option is changed.

1. Select After Effects > Preferences > Appearance (macOS) or Edit > Preferences > Appearance (Windows).

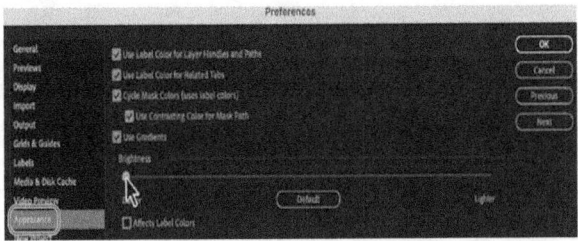

2. Watch the screen as it changes when you move the Brightness slider to the left or right.

3. Click Cancel to keep your preferences the same or OK to save the new brightness level. To return to the normal brightness level, click normal.

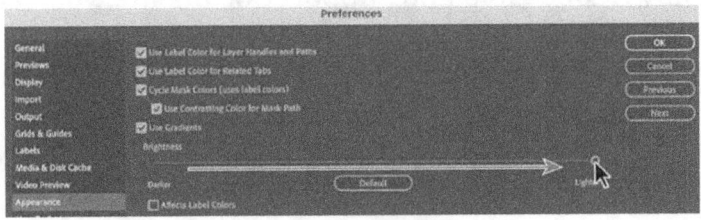

4. To save changes without closing the file, select File > Close Project.

Finding Resources for Using After Effects

Interactive tutorials are available within the After Effects product. Choose Learn from the Workspace bar to get to them. The Learn panel contains many interactive tutorials as well as an overview of the UI and key features.

The tutorials in the Learn panel and more advanced tutorials online are both easily accessible from the Home window that displays when you launch the application. To help you make the most of After Effects, it also offers links to additional resources. By selecting the Home icon located in the Tools panel, you can go back to the Home window at any moment.

Visit the Adobe website for detailed and current information about utilizing the After Effects panels, tools, and other application features. Simply type a search query into the Search Help box in the top right corner of the application window to get information in the After Effects Help and support papers, as well as on other websites important to After Effects users. To access only Adobe Help and support documents, you can filter the results.

CHAPTER 2: CREATING A BASIC ANIMATION USING EFFECTS AND PRESETS

Creating a New Composition

The steps are very simple. You need to import footage and create a new composition. After you've created a composition, you'll add your footage item to it.

Importing a background image

The background image will be imported first.

1. Navigate to the Assets folder in your Lessons/Lesson02 folder by selecting File > Import > File.

2. Click Import or Open after choosing the MauiCoast.jpg file.

Making an empty composition

You'll start by making the composition alone, without any layers.

1. One of the following actions will result in a new composition:

At the bottom of the Project panel, select the Create A New Composition button (Create A New Composition button icon).

In the Composition panel, click the New Composition button.

Select New Composition under Composition.

In Windows, press Ctrl+N, and in Mac OS, Command+N.

2. Do the following in the Composition Settings dialog box:

Name the composition explore Hawaii.

In the Preset pop-up menu, select HD, 1920x1080, and 29.97 frames per second. This preset automatically determines a high-definition video's width, height, pixel aspect ratio, and frame rate.

Type 300 to specify 3 seconds in the Duration area, then click OK.

Both the Composition panel and the Timeline panel in After Effects show an empty composition with the name Explore Hawaii. You will now include the background.

3. To include the MauiCoast.jpg footage item in the Explore Hawaii composition, drag it from the Project panel to the Timeline panel.

4. To scale the backdrop image to the size of the composition, pick the MauiCoast layer in the Timeline panel and then select Layer > Transform > Fit To Comp.

Importing the foreground element

Your backdrop is currently set up. You will utilize a layered Illustrator vector graphic as the foreground item.

1. Select File > Import > File.

2. Select the BlueCrabLogo.ai file from the Lessons/Lesson02/Assets folder in the Import File dialog box. (If file extensions are hidden, it is referred to as BlueCrabLogo.)

3. Composition can be selected from the Import As menu. (In macOS, you might have to click Options for the Import As menu to appear.) Click Import or Open after that.

The BlueCrabLogo composition from the Illustrator file is added to the Project panel. Also visible is a folder with the name BlueCrabLogo Layers. The three separate Illustrator file layers are located in this folder. If you'd want to view the contents of the folder, click the arrow to open it.

4. Drag the BlueCrabLogo composition file from the Project panel into the Timeline panel above the MauiCoast layer.

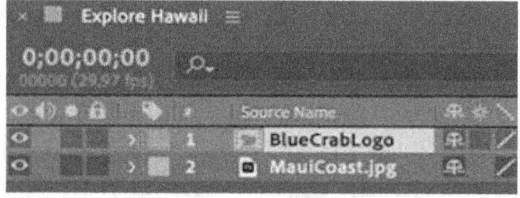

You should now see both the background image and the logo in the Composition panel and in the Timeline panel.

5. Choose File > Save to save your work so far.

Working With Imported Illustrator Layers

You must add text and animate the BlueCrabLogo design that was made in Illustrator using After Effects. You must open the BlueCrabLogo composition in its own Timeline and Composition panels in order to edit the layers of the Illustrator file separately from the backdrop video.

1. In the Project panel, double-click the BlueCrabLogo composition.

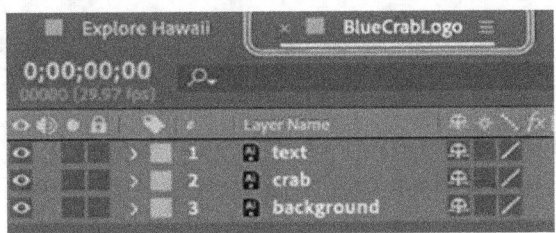

   The composition's Timeline and Composition panels appear when it is first opened.

2. Click on the Composition panel, choose the Horizontal Type tool (T) from the Tools panel, and then type.

3. Select all of the text you just entered, then type EXPLORE HAWAII in all capital letters. Observe how the generic Text 1 layer name in the Timeline panel is replaced with the text you typed, EXPLORE HAWAII.

Choose a sans serif typeface, such as Impact, and increase the font size to 80 pixels in the Character panel. To choose the yellow color, click the outer edge of the logo after clicking the eyedropper (Eyedropper icon) in the Character panel. It is applied to the text you wrote by After Effects. Maintain the default settings for all other choices in the Character panel.

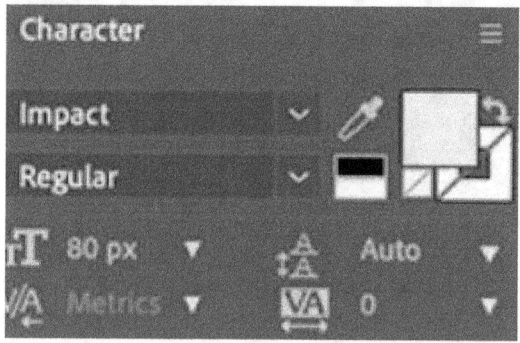

You'll use a guide to position the words you just typed.

4. In the Tools panel, click the Selection tool icon to choose it.

5. Drag a guide from the top ruler into the Composition panel after selecting View > Show Rulers.

6. In the Edit Value dialog box, enter 120 and click OK after right-clicking or controlling-clicking the guide and selecting Edit Position. When you specify a location, the guide moves there.

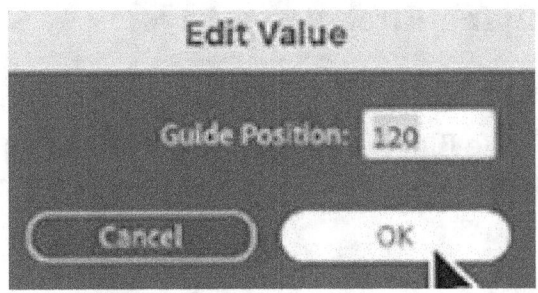

7. Snapping the bottom border of the text to the guide will center it over the image.

8. Another guide can be added by dragging it from the top ruler, right-clicking or controlling it, choosing Edit Position, entering 150 in the Edit Value dialog box, and choosing OK.

9. To select all three logo layers in the Timeline panel, first select the backdrop layer and then Shift-select the text layer. Align the lower guide and the top of the logo.

33

10. To see the ruler and the guides, select View > Show Rulers first, followed by View > Show Guides.

11. The Save option is found under File > Save.

Applying Effects to a Layer

Returning to the Explore Hawaii main composition, you will now add an effect to the BlueCrabLogo layer. By doing this, the effect will be applied to every layer inside the BlueCrabLogo composition.

1. Select the BlueCrabLogo layer by clicking the Explore Hawaii tab in the Timeline panel.

2. To view the Scale attribute, press S. scale is adjusted to 250%.

   Your next effect will only be applied to the logo's elements and not the background picture.

3. Effect > Perspective > Drop Shadow should be selected while the layer is still active.

The logo image and the phrases Explore Hawaii, which are nested layers of the BlueCrabLogo layer in the Composition panel, have a soft-edged shadow behind

34

them. Using the Effect Controls panel, you can alter the effect.

4. If the Effect Controls panel is not already open, select Window > Effect Controls. Make sure that the drop shadow's Distance is 5 and its Softness is 4 in the Effect Controls panel. Each value can be changed by dragging the blue value or by clicking the field and entering a number.

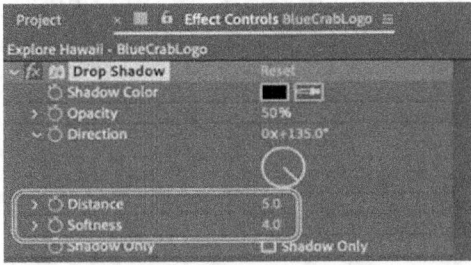

5. Click the Effects & Presets tab to open the panel. Then click the arrow next to Stylize to expand the category.

6. With the BlueCrabLogo layer selected in the Timeline panel, drag the Color Emboss effect into the Composition panel.

The Color Emboss effect sharpens the edges of objects in the layer without suppressing the original colors. The Effect Controls panel displays the Color Emboss effect and its settings below the Drop Shadow effect.

7. Choose File > Save to save your work.

Applying an Animation Preset

The type has been set in place and given various effects. You can utilize a straightforward preset that will fade the words "Explore Hawaii" into the screen next to the logo. To apply the animation to just the EXPLORE HAWAII text layer, you must edit the BlueCrabLogo composition.

1. Select the EXPLORE HAWAII layer by clicking the BlueCrabLogo tab in the Timeline panel.

2. You want the text to begin fading in at 1:05, so move the current-time indicator at that moment.

3. Select Animation Presets > Text > Animate In from the Effects & Presets window.

4. On the Explore Hawaii layer in the Timeline panel or over the words Explore Hawaii in the Composition panel, drag the Fade Up Words animation preset. You are viewing the first frame of the animation, before the words have begun to emerge, so don't worry about the text disappearing.

5. To manually preview the text animation, drag the time indicator to 2:10 and click a blank space in the Timeline

window to deselect the EXPLORE HAWAII layer. One word at a time, the text appears until the words Explore Hawaii are fully visible at 2:10.

Precomposing Layers for a New Animation

You probably can't wait to see a glimpse of the entire animation as the presentation graphic is progressing beautifully. But before you do, give every part of the logo—aside from the text "Explore Hawaii"—a dissolve. The text, crab, and background layers of the BlueCrabLogo composition must be precomposed in order to accomplish this.

Precomposing allows layers to be nested inside of a composition. The layers are precomposed to a new composition, which replaces the specified layers. Precomposing is a simple approach to quickly establish intermediate levels of nesting in an existing hierarchy when you wish to change the order in which layer components are presented.

1. In the BlueCrabLogo Timeline window, shift-click to choose the text, crab, and background layers.

2. Select Pre-compose under Layer.

3. Give the new composition the name Dissolve_logo in the Pre-compose dialog box. Ensure that the option to Move All Attributes Into The New Composition is chosen. then press OK.

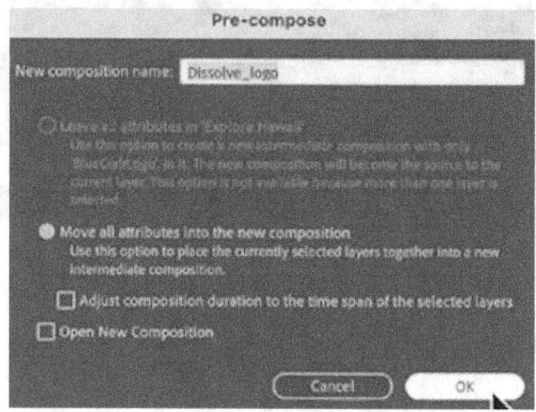

4. In the Timeline panel, make sure the Dissolve_logo layer is selected, then press the Home key or move the current time indicator to 0:00.

5. Drag the Dissolve - Vapor animation preset onto the Dissolve_logo layer in the Timeline panel or onto the Composition panel by selecting it in the Animation Presets > Transitions - Dissolves section of the Effects & Presets panel.

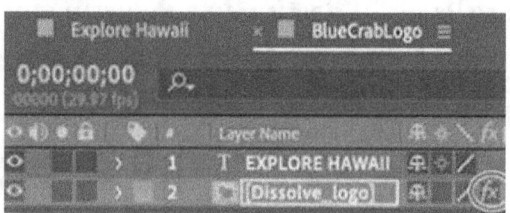

6. Choose File > Save.

Adding Transparency

During the presentation, the logo should be visible in a corner of the frame. To make the logo suitable for this use, you must decrease its opacity, scale it, and move it.

1. Go to 2:10 while you're still in the Explore Hawaii Timeline screen.

2. By selecting it and pressing T, the BlueCrabLogo layer's Opacity attribute will be shown. The Opacity is 100%— completely opaque—by default. To set an Opacity keyframe at this moment, click the stopwatch symbol (Stopwatch icon).

3. To move to the end of the time ruler (2:29), press the End key or drag the current-time indication. Then, set the Opacity to 40%. A keyframe is added by After Effects.

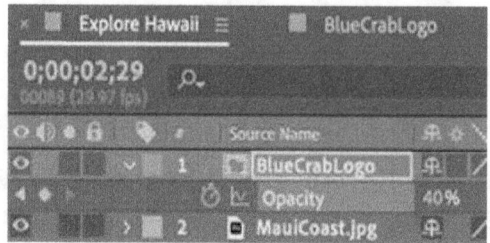

4. Press P to show the Position property at 2:10 and Shift+S to show the Scale property as well. To set the first keyframes for both attributes, click the stopwatch icons (Stopwatch symbol).

5. Change the Scale to 60% and the Position to 1700, 935 at 2:25.

6. To preview your composition, press the spacebar, enter 0 on your numeric keypad, or click the Play button (Play/Stop button icon) in the Preview panel.

7. When you're done, press the spacebar to halt the playing.

8. To save your project, select File > Save.

Rendering the Composition

You are prepared to write the introduction of your presentation. The layers of a composition, along with the masks, effects, and properties of each layer, are rendered frame by frame into one or more output files, or, in the case of an image sequence, into a string of related files, when you create output.

Your final composition's frame size, quality, complexity, and compression technique will all affect how long it takes to create a movie from it. Your composition becomes a render item using the render parameters you've specified it when you add it to the render queue.

The format you select for rendering output from After Effects relies on the platform from which you'll play your finished product or on the specifications of your hardware, such as a video-editing machine. After Effects offers a range of formats and compression techniques.

To make the composition suitable for television transmission, you must render and export it.

1. To advance the Project panel, click the Project tab. Select Window > Project to reveal the Project tab if it is hidden.

2. To add the composition to the render queue, choose one of the following:

Select the Explore Hawaii composition in the Project panel, and choose Composition > Add To Render Queue. The Render Queue panel opens automatically.

Choose Window > Render Queue to open the Render Queue panel, and then drag the Explore Hawaii composition from the Project panel onto the Render Queue panel.

3. To view more Render Settings choices, click the arrow. After Effects generates compositions by default in Full Resolution and Best Quality. For this project, the default parameters are adequate.

4. The Output Module selections will expand once you click the arrow. The produced composition is encoded into a video file by After Effects using the H.264 - Match Render Settings - 15Mbps preset by default.

5. To open the Output To menu, click the blue words.

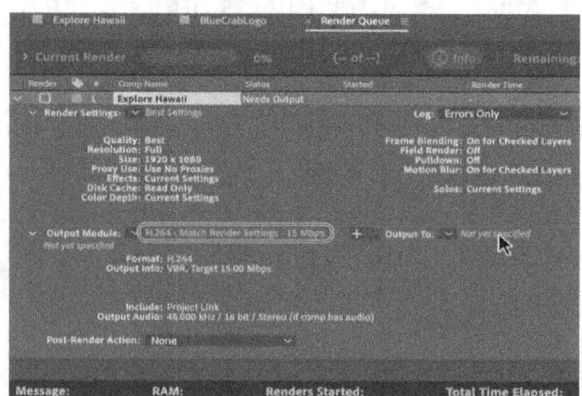

6. Accept the default movie title (Explore Hawaii), choose the Lessons/Lesson02/Finished_Project folder as the

output location, and then click Save in the Output Movie To dialog box.

7. Click the Render button once more in the Render Queue screen.

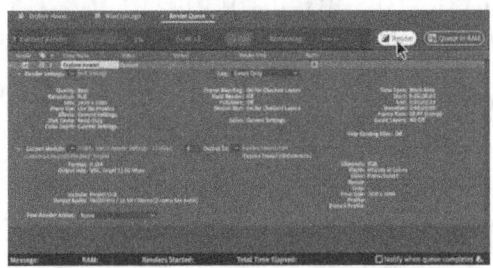

While encoding the file, After Effects shows a progress meter in the Render Queue panel. When all items in the Render Queue have been rendered and encoded, an audio alert is played.

8. Double-click the Explore Hawaii.mp4 file in the Lessons/Lesson02/Finished_Project folder to launch Windows Media Player or QuickTime, and then play the video to view your finished project.

9. After saving and closing the project file, end your After Effects session.

CHAPTER 3: ANIMATING TEXT

About Text Layers

You can precisely and flexibly add text in After Effects. Numerous text controls are available in the Tools, Character, and Paragraph panels. In the Composition panel, you may rapidly modify the text's font, style, size, and color as well as generate and edit horizontal or vertical text. Alignment, justification, and word-wrapping are just a few of the formatting settings that can be applied to specific characters and adjusted for full paragraphs. In addition to all of these styling options, After Effects offers capabilities for quickly animating particular characters and elements, like text color and opacity.

Point text and paragraph text are the two types of text used in After Effects. To input and format text as one or more paragraphs, use paragraph text; use point text to enter a single word or line of characters.

Text layers in After Effects resemble other levels in many ways. Text layers can be animated, given 3D layer designations, given effects and expressions, and edited while being viewed from different perspectives. Text layers are continually rasterized, just like layers imported from Illustrator, so that when the layer is scaled or resized, the text keeps its sharp, resolution-independent edges. The ability to animate text in a text layer using unique text-animator attributes and selectors, as well as the inability to open a text layer in its own Layer panel, are the two key distinctions between text layers and other layers.

Installing a Font Using Adobe Fonts

Through Adobe Fonts, which is a part of an Adobe Creative Cloud subscription, you may access hundreds of different fonts. Installing a font that will be suitable for the title text will be done using Adobe Fonts. Any application can use an Adobe Fonts typeface that you have installed on your computer.

1. Select File > Adobe Fonts From Here.

    Your default browser is launched by After Effects with the Adobe Fonts page.

2. Ensure that Creative Cloud is registered to you. If not, enter your Adobe ID after clicking Sign In at the top of the screen.

3. In the example text area, type Snorkel Tours. Move the slider to adjust the font size if you can't read all of it.

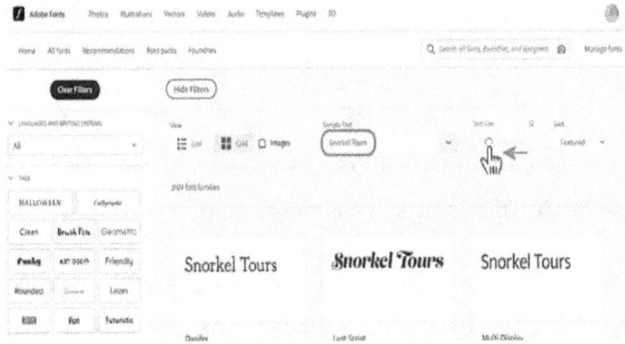

Your own text can be used as the sample text so that you can see how a typeface will appear in your project.

On the Adobe Fonts website, you can explore fonts, but because there are so many, it's frequently more effective to filter them or search for a particular type. To choose fonts that fit your needs, you'll filter the list.

4. Choose Name from the Sort menu in the upper right corner. Then, on the left side of the page, hide the Tags area, and select Sans Serif in the Classification area. In the Properties area, select the buttons for medium weight, medium width, medium x-height, low contrast, and standard capitalization.

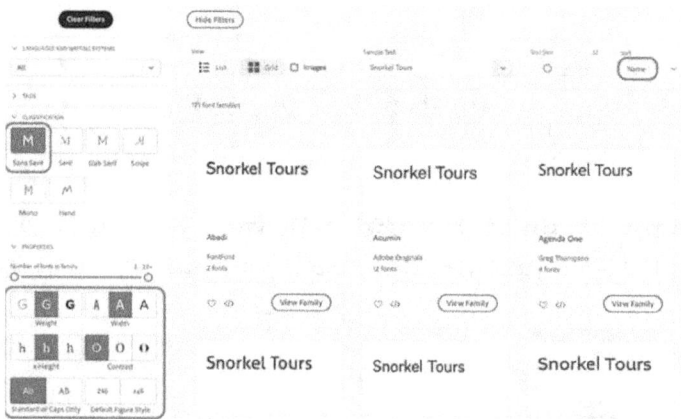

Adobe Fonts displays several fonts that meet the requirements you specified.

5. Browse a few pages' worth of fonts to see what's available. Calluna Sans, which is probably on the third page, will work nicely.

6. Click Calluna Sans.

For each font in the chosen family, Adobe Fonts shows an image with the typeface used in it, some sample text, and further information.

7. Next to the Regular and Bold font styles, click Activate Font.

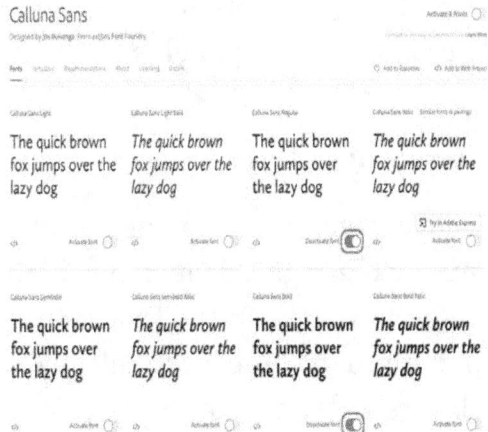

The chosen typefaces are automatically installed on your computer and made accessible in all programs, including After Effects. Close Adobe Fonts and your browser once you've set your fonts to active.

Creating and Formatting Point Text

Each line of text entered as point text in After Effects is autonomous; as you alter the text, the length of a line changes but does not automatically wrap to the next line. Your text is displayed in a new text layer. The location of the text baseline is shown by the thin line through the I-beam.

1. Select the Horizontal Type tool (Horizontal Type tool icon) from the Tools panel.

2. Type "Snorkel Tours" anywhere in the Composition panel by clicking. Enter on the number keypad or click the layer name in the Timeline panel to leave text editing mode. The Composition panel is set to the text layer.

Using the Character panel

Options for formatting characters can be found in the Character panel. When text is highlighted, just the highlighted text is affected by changes you make in the Character panel. Changes made in the Character panel effect the selected text layers and, if any, the text layers' selected Source Text keyframes, even if no text is highlighted. Changes you make in the Character panel become the defaults for the subsequent text entry if neither any text is highlighted nor any text layers are selected.

1. Each font's sample text is shown in After Effects. You can filter fonts to just show Adobe fonts or your favorite fonts.

2. In the Timeline panel, select the Snorkel Tours text layer.

3. Select Calluna Sans Bold from the Font Family menu in the Character panel.

4. Make sure there isn't a stroke selected and set the font size to 90 pixels.

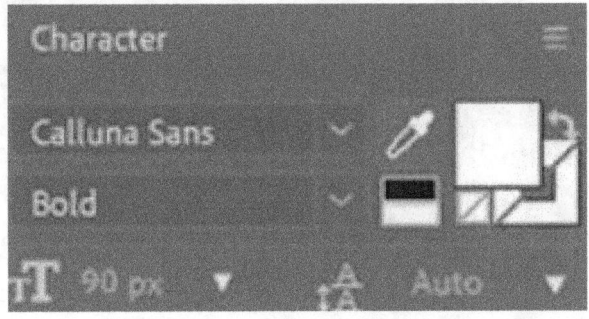

Maintain the default values for all other parameters.

Using the Paragraph panel

Alignment, indentation, and leading are just a few examples of parameters that can be configured in the paragraph panel to apply to the entire paragraph. Each line in point text is treated as a single paragraph. Setting formatting choices for a single paragraph, a group of paragraphs, or all paragraphs in a text layer can be done using the paragraph panel. There is only one change that has to be made to the title text of this composition in the Paragraph panel.

1. Select "Center Text" from the Paragraph panel's buttons. Instead of the composition's center, this aligns horizontal text to the layer's center.

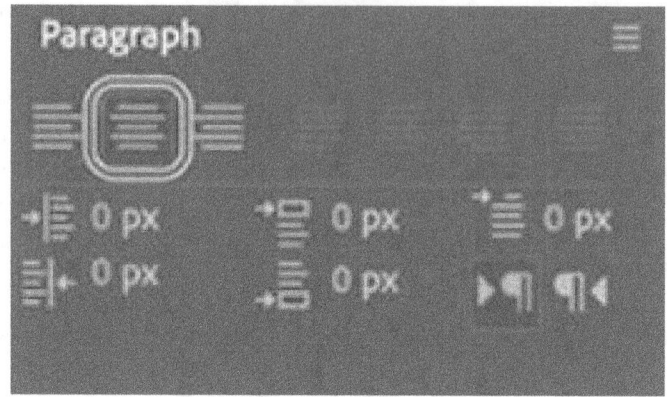

2. Leave all other options at their default settings.

Positioning the type

In the Composition panel, you can display rulers, guides, and grids to precisely arrange layers, such as the text layer you're working on right now. These visual aids for referencing are absent from the rendered movie.

1. Make sure the Timeline panel has the Snorkel Tours text layer selected.

2. Select Fit To Comp Width under Layer > Transform. This scales the layer to match the composition's width.

The text layer can now be positioned using a grid.

3. Select View > Snap To Grid after selecting View > Show Grid.

4. Using the Selection tool (Selection tool icon), drag the text up in the Composition panel until the text is in the top quarter of the composition, centered in the surface of the water. Press Shift after you start dragging to constrain the movement and help you position the text.

5. When the layer is in position, choose View > Show Grid again to hide the grid.

   This project isn't destined for broadcast TV, so it's okay that the title extends beyond the title-safe and action-safe areas of the composition at the beginning of the animation.

6. Choose File > Save to save your project.

Animating With Scale Keyframes

When you used the Fit To Comp Width command on the text layer earlier in this session, it was scaled to about 250% of its original size. The layer's scale will now be animated such that the type gradually decreases to 200%.

1. Set the current time indicator in the Timeline panel to 3:00.

2. Pressing the S key will expose the layer's Scale property when the Snorkel Tours text layer is selected.

3. To add a Scale keyframe at the current time (3:00), click the stopwatch symbol.

4. Move the current-time indicator to 5:00.

5. Reduce the scale settings of the layer to 200 and 200%. At this moment, After Effects creates a new Scale keyframe.

Previewing a range of frames

You'll now see a preview of the animation. You only need to watch the first five seconds of the composition because that is when the text animation starts, even though the composition lasts 13 seconds.

1. Set the end of the work area by dragging the current time indication to 5:10 and pressing N. Just before 5:10, the scale animation comes to an end.

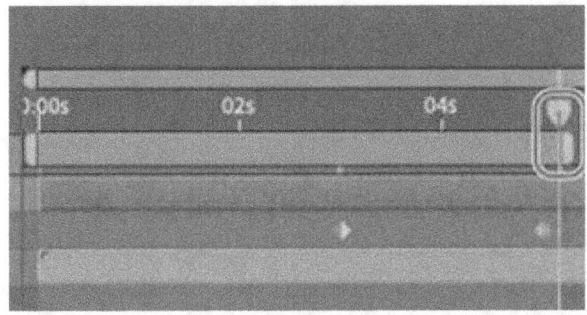

2. To preview the animation from 0:00 to 5:10, press the spacebar. The movie's name shrinks in size.

3. Once you've seen the animation, press the spacebar to halt playback.

Using a text animation preset

The title currently displays at the start of the video. To make the title's appearance more intriguing, you'll animate it. Utilizing one of the many animation presets included with After Effects is the simplest method to accomplish that. An animation preset can be modified after application and saved for later usage in different projects.

1. To ensure that the current-time indicator is at the start of the time ruler, press the Home key or navigate to 0:00.

   The current time's animation settings are used by After Effects.

2. Choose the Text Layer for Snorkel Tours.

Browsing Animation Presets

1. To view presets, select Animation > Browse. The After Effects Presets folder's contents are shown in Adobe Bridge once it is opened. If prompted, select Yes to enable Bridge's After Effects addon.

2. Double-click the Text folder in the Content window, followed by the Organic folder.

3. Click to choose Autumn, the first preset. In the Preview window of Adobe Bridge, a sample of the animation is played.

4. Watch a couple additional presets on the Preview panel by selecting them.

5. Right-click (Windows) or Control-click (MacOS) the thumbnail and select Place > In Adobe After Effects 2023 after previewing the Ripple preset.

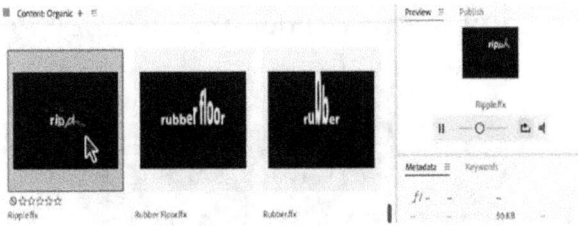

6. Go back to After Effects while keeping Adobe Bridge open in the background.

The Snorkel Tours layer is selected in After Effects and given the preset, but the layer is no longer visible in the composition. This is so that the letters can't yet be seen in the scene at 0:00, the first frame of the animation.

Customizing an animation preset

All of a layer's characteristics and keyframes are presented in the Timeline panel once you apply an animation preset to it. These attributes will be used to alter the preset.

1. To view an animation preview, press the spacebar. The headline then shrinks to 200% as the letters flip into position. To halt the preview, press the spacebar once again.

The background seems to ripple into the lettering. It looks amazing, but to modify the arrangement of the characters, you must adjust the default

2. Expand the layer's attributes after selecting the Snorkel Tours text layer in the Timeline panel. Go to the

Advanced properties under Text > Animator - Ripple 1 (Skew) > Selector Offset.

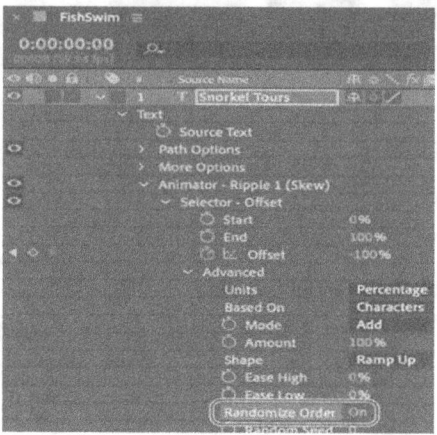

3. To enable the Randomize Order feature, simply click on the Cick Off button next to it.

The Randomize Order property alters the sequence in which letters appear on the screen, creating a ripple effect.

4. To preview the edited animation manually, drag the current-time indicator from 0:00 to 3:00.

5. To hide the properties of the layer, you can choose to hide them.

6. To move the current-time indicator to the end of the time ruler, press the End key, and then press N to set the end bracket of the work area.

7. To reset the current-time indicator to the beginning of the time ruler, either press the Home key or navigate to 0:00.

8. To save your project, go to the File menu and choose Save.

Importing text

You will now import the remaining text for this composition from a layered Photoshop file.

To do this, follow these steps:

1. Open the Import File dialog box by double-clicking on an empty area in the Project panel.

2. In the dialog box, select the LOCATION.psd file located in the Lessons/Lesson03/Assets folder. From the Import As menu, choose Composition – Retain Layer Sizes. (On macOS, you may need to click Options to see the Import As menu.) Then click Import or Open.

3. In the LOCATION.psd dialog box, select Editable Layer Styles and click OK.

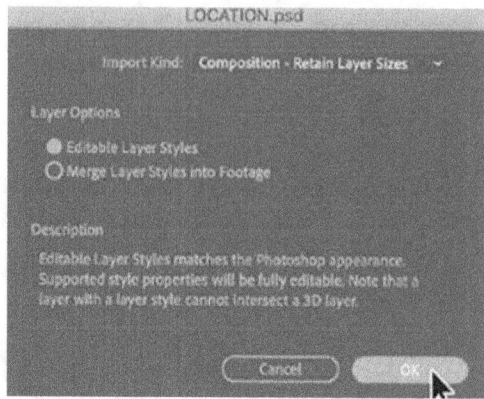

After Effects has the ability to import Photoshop layer styles, preserving the appearance of the layers being imported. The imported file will be added as a composition in the Project panel, and its layers will be organized within a separate folder.

4. Next, drag the LOCATION composition from the Project panel and place it at the top of the layer stack in the Timeline panel.

Since you imported the LOCATION.psd file as a composition with its layers intact, you can now work on it in its own Timeline panel. This allows you to edit and animate the layers independently.

58

Editing imported text

Currently, the imported text in After Effects cannot be edited. However, you can change this to have control over the type and apply animations. The LOCATION.psd file serves as a standard template for indicating the locations of company tours. In order to make it more noticeable for this promotion, you will modify the text and add a stroke effect.

Follow these steps:

1. Open the LOCATION composition by double-clicking on it in the Project panel. This will open it in its own Timeline panel.

2. In the Timeline panel, select the LOCATION layer and go to Layer > Create > Convert To Editable Text. If you encounter a warning about missing fonts, click OK.

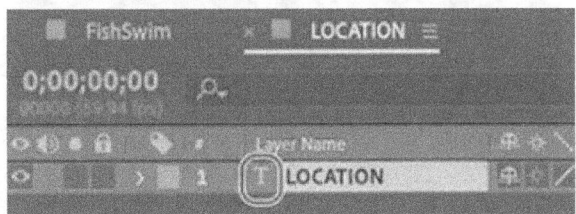

Now, the text layer can be edited, allowing you to customize the tour location.

3. Double-click the LOCATION layer in the Timeline panel to select the text. This action will automatically switch to the Horizontal Type tool (represented by the Horizontal Type tool icon).

4. Enter "ISLA MUJERES" using the keyboard while the text is selected.

5. Switch to the Selection tool (represented by the Selection tool icon) to exit text-editing mode.

6. If the Character panel is not open, go to Window > Character to open it.

7. Click on the Stroke color box to select it, then click on it again to open the Text Color dialog box. Choose a teal blue color (with RGB values of R=70, G=92, B=101), and click OK. Keep the other settings unchanged.

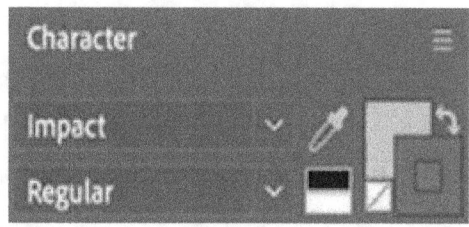

8. Save your progress so far by selecting File > Save.

Animating text to appear over time

To create an organic flow of the letters of the location, "ISLA MUJERES," onto the screen under the activity title, you can utilize a text animation preset. Here's how:

1. Go to the 5:00 mark on the timeline, where the title has completed scaling to its final size.

2. Select the LOCATION layer in the Timeline panel.

3. Press Ctrl+Alt+Shift+O (Windows) or Command+Option+Shift+O (macOS) to switch to Adobe Bridge.

4. Navigate to the Presets/Text/Animate In folder.

5. Choose the Raining Characters In animation preset and preview it in the Preview panel. This preset gradually reveals the text, which suits your purpose.

6. Right-click or Control-click the Raining Characters In preset and select "Place In Adobe After Effects 2023" to apply it to the LOCATION layer. Then, return to After Effects.

7. With the LOCATION layer selected in the Timeline panel, press UU to view the properties modified by the animation preset. You should observe two keyframes for Range Selector 1 Offset: one at 5:00 and another at 7:15.

8. Go to the 6:00 mark and drag the second Range Selector 1 Offset keyframe to 6:00.

9. Select the LOCATION layer and press U to hide the modified properties.

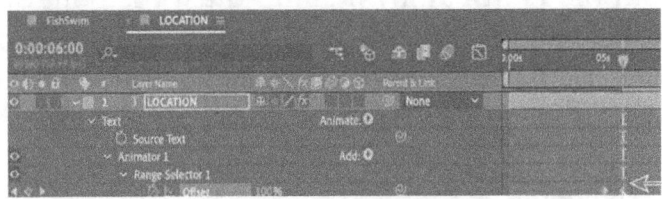

10. Make the FishSwim tab active in the Timeline panel, and if needed, go to the 6:00 mark.

11. Use the Selection tool (represented by the Selection tool icon) to move the LOCATION layer, aligning ISLA MUJERES to the right and just below Snorkel Tours.

12. Deselect all layers. Drag the current-time indicator from 4:00 to 6:00 on the time ruler to witness the letters falling into place. Then, save your progress.

Animating Type Tracking

The company name will then be added, and its look will be animated using a text animation tracking preset. Words can appear to extend outward as they come onscreen from a central point by animating tracking.

Applying a tracking preset

First, begin by creating the text. Then, add a tracking preset.

1. Start by selecting the Horizontal Type tool (rT). Proceed to type "BLUE CRAB CHARTERS".

2. Next, choose the BLUE CRAB CHARTERS layer. Within the Character panel, select "Times New Roman Bold" from the Font Family menu. Adjust the Font Size to 48 px, set the fill to white, and ensure the stroke is set to none. In the Paragraph panel, make sure to select Center Text.

3. Navigate to the time 7:10.

4. To move the BLUE CRAB CHARTERS layer to the lower third of the screen, aligned with Snorkel Tours, use the

Selection tool (represented by the Selection tool icon), as shown in the provided image.

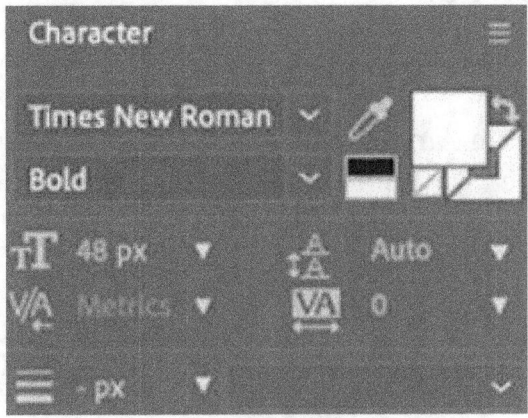

5. Access the Effects & Presets panel. Type "Increase Tracking" in the search box and double-click on the preset to apply it to the BLUE CRAB CHARTERS layer.

6. Manually preview the tracking animation by dragging the current-time indicator across the time ruler between 7:10 and 9:10.

Customizing the tracking animation preset

The text needs to expand, but initially, you want the letters to be extremely close to each other, almost overlapping, and then gradually expand to a reasonable and readable distance. Additionally, the animation needs to be faster. To achieve both objectives, you will adjust the Tracking Amount.

1. Begin by selecting the BLUE CRAB CHARTERS layer in the Timeline panel. To reveal the modified properties, press UU.

2. Navigate to the time 7:10.

3. Within Animator 1, modify the Tracking Amount to -5, which will squeeze the letters together closely.

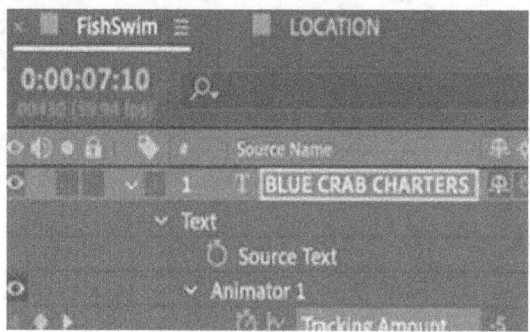

4. Click on the Go To Next Keyframe arrow, denoted by the Go to Next Keyframe arrow icon, for the Tracking Amount property. Then change the value to 0.

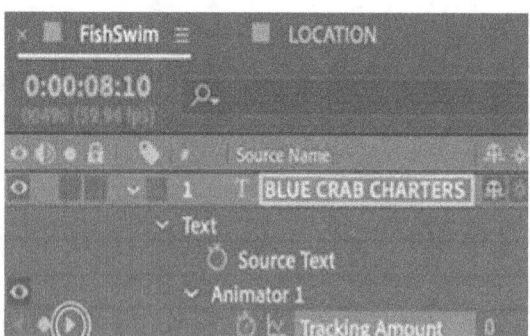

5. Drag the current-time indicator across the time ruler between 7:10 and 8:10. This will result in the letters

expanding and the animation coming to a halt at the last keyframe.

6. Finally, hide the properties for all layers.

Animating Text Opacity

To enhance the animation of the company name, you can add a fading effect as the letters expand. To achieve this, you will animate the Opacity property of the layer.

1. Ensure that the BLUE CRAB CHARTERS layer is selected.

2. Press T to reveal only the Opacity property of the layer.

3. Go to the time 7:10 and set the Opacity to 0%. Then, click on the stopwatch icon to set an Opacity keyframe.

4. Move to the time 7:20 and set the Opacity to 100%. After Effects will automatically add a second keyframe.

   Now, as the letters expand onscreen, the company name will gradually fade in.

5. Drag the current-time indicator across the time ruler between 7:10 and 8:10 to observe the letters of the company name fading in as they spread out.

6. To create a smooth easing effect at the end, right-click (Windows) or Control-click (macOS) the final Opacity keyframe and select Keyframe Assistant > Easy Ease In.

7. Finally, save your file by choosing File > Save.

Animating an Image to Replace Text

You have utilized various animation presets to modify the appearance of text onscreen. Now, you will employ one to make text disappear and replace it with an imported logo. The logo will be animated to swoop in and erase the "BLUE CRAB CHARTERS" text.

Animating an important image

1. To get started, click on the Project tab to bring the Project panel forward. Double-click on an empty area within the Project panel, and the Import File dialog box will open.

2. Locate and select the BlueCrabLogo.psd file in the Lessons/Lesson03/Assets folder. From the Import As menu, choose "Composition – Retain Layer Sizes." (On macOS, you may need to click on Options to access the Import As menu.) Then, click on Import or Open.

3. In the BlueCrabLogo.psd dialog box, select "Editable Layer Styles" and click OK.

4. Drag the BlueCrabLogo composition into the Timeline panel, positioning it at the top of the layer stack.

   Although the logo is currently centered on the screen, your intention is for it to enter from the left and move downward to replace the "Blue Crab Charters" text. To achieve this effect, you will animate the layer's Position and Scale properties.

66

5. Move the current-time indicator to 10:00.

6. With the BlueCrabLogo layer selected, press P to reveal its Position property. Press Shift+S to also reveal the Scale property.

7. Adjust the Position values to -810, 122, and set the Scale to 25%. Then, click on the stopwatch icon next to each of these properties to create initial keyframes.

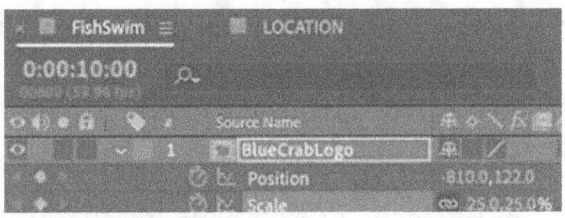

8. Go to 11:00 and change the Position to 377, 663, and the Scale to 85%. This will generate keyframes for these properties in After Effects.

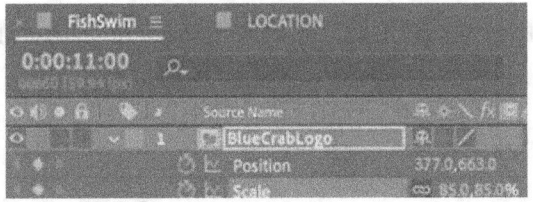

Although the logo now moves into position, you want it to swoop in rather than moving in a straight line. To achieve this, you will add some intermediate Position keyframes.

9. Go to 10:15 and modify the Position to 139, 633.

10. Go to 10:30 and adjust the Position to 675, 633.

11. Return to 10:00 and press the spacebar to preview the animation. Press the spacebar again to stop the preview, and then hide all layer properties.

Applying an animation preset

Now, it's time to make it appear as though the logo is erasing the text as it arrives by applying an animation preset.

1. Go to 10:10 and select the BLUE CRAB CHARTERS layer.

2. In the Effects & Presets panel, search for "Fade Out By Character".

3. Double-click on the "Fade Out By Character" preset to apply it to the layer.

4. With the BLUE CRAB CHARTERS layer selected, press U to view its animated properties.

5. Move to 10:12.

6. Adjust the first Range Selector 1: Start keyframe to 10:12.

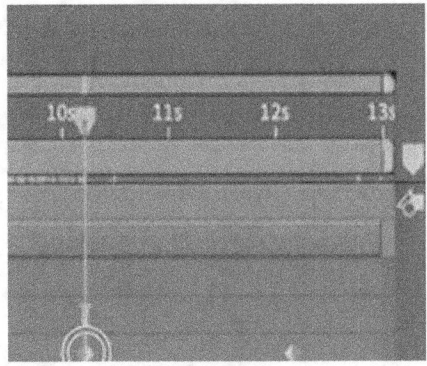

7. Go to 10:29 and modify the second Range Selector 1: Start keyframe to 10:29.

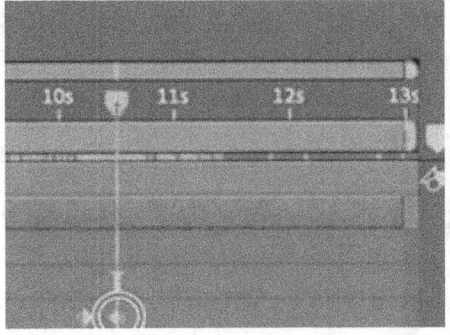

8. Press the spacebar to preview your project, and then press the spacebar again to stop the preview.

9. Press U to hide the layer properties and save your work.

Using a text animator group

Text animator groups provide the ability to animate individual letters within a block of text in a layer. In this case, you will use a text animator group to draw attention to the word "BLUE

69

CRAB CHARTERS" by animating only the characters in the middle word, without affecting the tracking and opacity animation of the other characters in the layer.

1. In the Timeline panel, navigate to 9:10.

2. Expand the layer named "BLUE CRAB CHARTERS" to reveal its Text property group name.

3. Select the "BLUE CRAB CHARTERS" layer, ensuring that only the layer name is selected.

4. Next to the Text property group name, click on the Animate pop-up menu and choose "Skew".

   After Effects will add a property group named "Animator 3" to the layer's Text properties.

5. Select "Animator 3", press Enter or Return, and rename it as "Skew Animator". Press Enter or Return again to confirm the new name.

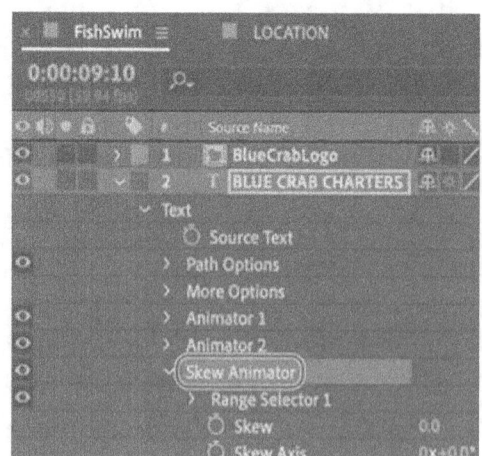

Now, you are ready to define the range of letters that you want to skew.

6. Expand the properties of the "Skew Animator's Range Selector 1".

Each animator group comes with a default range selector, which allows you to specify the letters to be animated. You can add additional selectors to an animator group or apply multiple animator properties to the same range selector.

7. While observing the Composition panel, drag the "Skew Animator's Range Selector 1 Start" value upwards (to the right) until the left selector indicator is positioned just before the letter "C" in "CRAB".

8. Drag the "Skew Animator's Range Selector 1 End" value downwards (to the left) until its indicator is placed just after the letter "B" in "CRAB" in the Composition panel.

Now, any properties that you animate with the "Skew Animator" will only affect the selected characters.

Skewing the range of text

Now, you'll create a shaking and shimmying effect for the middle word by setting Skew keyframes.

1. Drag the Skew value of the Skew Animator left and right, and observe that only the selected word sways while the other words remain steady.

2. Set the Skew value of the Skew Animator to 0.

3. Go to 9:15 and click the stopwatch icon for Skew to add a keyframe to the property.

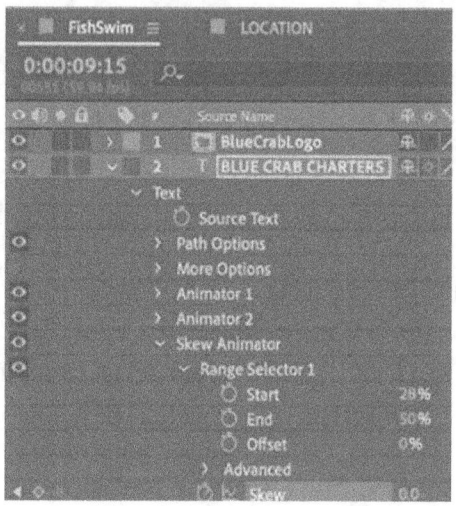

4. Move to 9:18 and set the Skew value to 50. After Effects adds a keyframe.

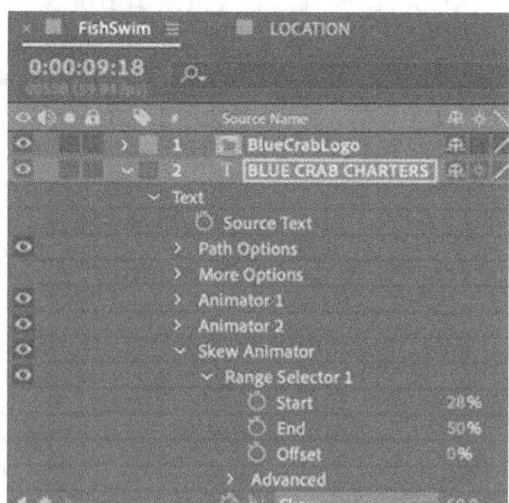

5. Navigate to 9:25 and change the Skew value to -50. Another keyframe is added.

6. Advance to 10:00 and set the Skew value to 0 to establish the final keyframe.

7. Click the Skew property name to select all Skew keyframes, then go to Animation > Keyframe Assistant > Easy Ease to apply Easy Ease to all keyframes.

8. Hide the properties for the BLUE CRAB CHARTERS layer in the Timeline panel.

9. Press Home or go to 0:00, and then preview the entire composition.

10. Press the spacebar to halt playback, and then select File > Save to save your work.

Animating a layer's position

1. In the FishSwim Timeline panel, navigate to 11:30.

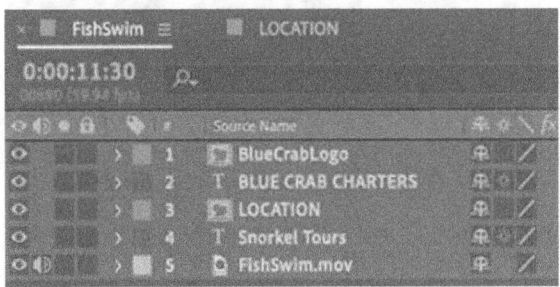

At this point, all the other text is on screen, allowing you to accurately position the "Providing Excursions Daily" line.

2. Select the Horizontal Type tool.

3. Ensure that no layers are selected, then click in the Composition panel in an area that doesn't overlap an existing text layer.

4. Type "Providing Excursions Daily."

5. Select the Providing Excursions Daily layer. In the Character panel, choose Calluna Sans Bold from the Font Family menu. Set the Font Size to 48 px.

6. In the Character panel, ensure that the Fill Color box is set to white.

7. Enable Small Caps. Keep all other options at their default settings.

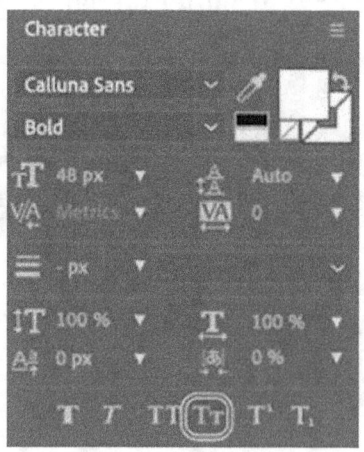

8. Select the Selection tool, then drag the Providing Excursions Daily layer so that the text aligns with the bottom of the logo and the right edge of Snorkel Tours.

9. Press P to display the layer's Position property, and click the stopwatch icon to create an initial keyframe for the layer.

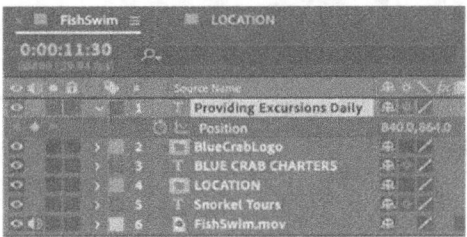

10. Go to 11:00, the point where the logo has replaced the company name.

11. Drag the Providing Excursions Daily layer off the right edge of the composition, holding the Shift key while dragging to create a straight path.

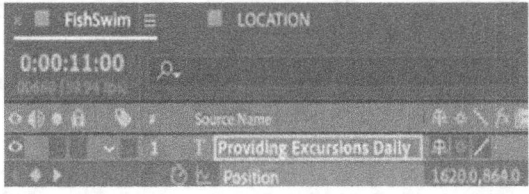

12. Preview the animation, then hide the Position property.

The result is a simple yet effective animation where the text moves in from the right side and stops in its final position next to the logo.

Chapter 4: Working With Shape Layers

Creating the Composition

First, you'll import the footage and create the composition.

1. Click on "New Composition From Footage" in the Composition panel.

2. Navigate to the Lessons/Lesson04/Assets folder on your hard disk and select the Background.mov file, then click Import or Open.

   After Effects adds the Background.mov file to the Project panel and creates a composition based on it. The new composition is opened in both the Timeline and Composition panels.

3. Press the spacebar to preview the background movie. Watch as the scene transitions from night to day with the sky brightening and the colors becoming more vibrant. Press the spacebar again to stop playback.

Adding a shape layer

After Effects provides five shape tools: Rectangle, Rounded Rectangle, Ellipse, Polygon, and Star. Drawing a shape directly in the Composition panel creates a new shape layer in the composition. You can customize stroke and fill settings, adjust the shape's path, and apply animation presets. All shape attributes are displayed in the Timeline panel, and each setting can be animated over time.

The same drawing tools can also create masks. Masks are used to hide or reveal areas on layers or serve as inputs for effects. Shapes, on the other hand, have their own dedicated layers. When you select a drawing tool, you can specify whether you want to draw a shape or a mask.

Drawing a shape

Begin by drawing a star.

1. Press the Home key or move the current-time indicator to the beginning of the time ruler.

2. Press F2 or click on an empty area in the Timeline panel to ensure that no layers are selected.

If you draw a shape while a layer is selected, it becomes a mask for that layer, indicated by a masked box cursor when you start drawing. If no layer is selected, After Effects creates a shape layer, and you'll see a star cursor when you begin drawing.

3. Go to Edit > Preferences > General (Windows) or After Effects > Preferences > General (macOS). Select "Center Anchor Point In New Shape Layers" and click OK.

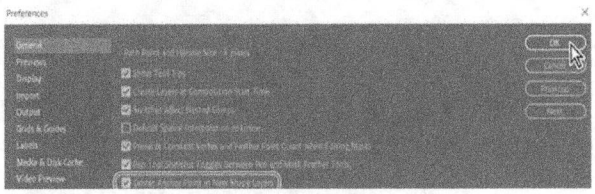

The anchor point is the reference point used by After Effects when it modifies a layer's position, scale, or rotation. By default, the anchor point of a shape layer is at the center of the composition. Enabling "Center Anchor Point In New Shape Layers" ensures that the anchor point is positioned at the center of the first shape you draw on a layer.

4. Select the Star tool, which is hidden behind the Rectangle tool in the Tools panel.

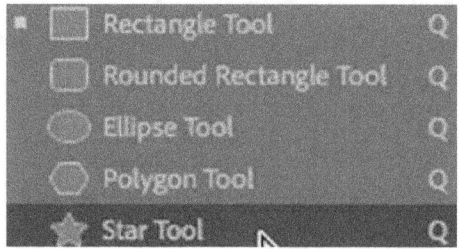

5. Draw a small star in the sky. The star shape will appear in the Composition panel, and After Effects will add a shape layer named "Shape Layer 1" to the Timeline panel.

6. Select the layer named "Shape Layer 1," press Enter or Return, and change the layer name to "Star 1." Press Enter or Return again to confirm the name change.

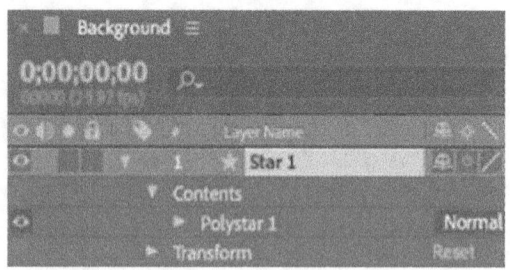

Apply fill and stroke

1. Select the "Star 1" layer in the Timeline panel.

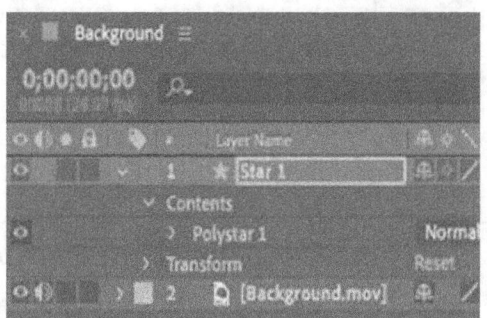

2. Click on the Fill Color box to open the Shape Fill Color dialog box.

3. Change the color to a bright yellow (e.g., R=215, G=234, B=23) and click OK.

4. Click on the Stroke Color box, change the stroke color to an even brighter yellow (e.g., R=252, G=245, B=3), and click OK.

5. Ensure that the Stroke Width value is set to 2 px.

6. Save your work so far by chooses File > Save.

Creating a self animating shape

Wiggle Paths is a path operation that transforms a smooth shape into a series of jagged peaks and valleys. It will be used to create a subtle shimmer effect for the star. Since it's a self-animating operation, you only need to modify a few properties to make the entire shape move on its own.

1. If the Star 1 layer is not already expanded in the Timeline panel, expand it. Then, select "Wiggle Paths" from the Add pop-up menu.

2. Press the spacebar to play the movie and observe the effect. Press the spacebar again to stop playback. However, the edges of the star appear too jagged, so we'll adjust the settings for a more subtle effect.

3. Expand the Wiggle Paths 1 properties. Change the Size to 2.0 and the Detail to 3.0.

4. Set the Wiggles/Second value to 5.0.

5. Click the Motion Blur switch for the layer to enable motion blur.

6. Hide the layer properties.

7. Press the spacebar to preview the effect of the shimmering star, and press it again to stop playback.

8. Move the current-time indicator to the beginning of the time ruler by pressing the Home key or manually dragging it.

9. Select the Star 1 layer and press T to reveal its Opacity property.

10. Click the stopwatch icon to create an initial keyframe with 100% opacity.

11. Go to the 2:15 mark, and change the Opacity value to 0%.

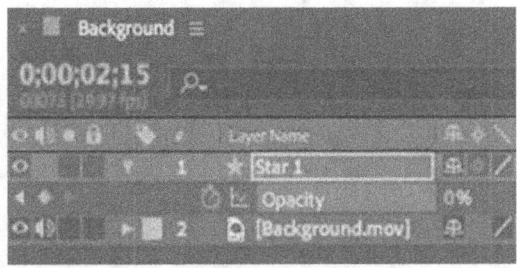

12. With the Star 1 layer selected, press T again to hide the Opacity property.

Duplicating a shape

The sky should contain multiple stars, all of which should shine. To achieve this, you will duplicate the original star multiple times, ensuring that each new layer possesses the same characteristics as the original. Subsequently, you will individually modify the position and rotation of each star. Lastly, you will animate the offset paths to enhance the twinkling effect.

1. To begin, press the Home key or move the current-time indicator to the start of the time ruler.

2. Locate the Star 1 layer in the Timeline panel and select it. Proceed to choose Edit > Duplicate.

3. After Effects will generate a new layer called Star 2 at the top of the layer stack, which will be an exact replica of the Star 1 layer, including its position.

4. To create five more star layers, press Ctrl+D (Windows) or Command+D (macOS) five times.

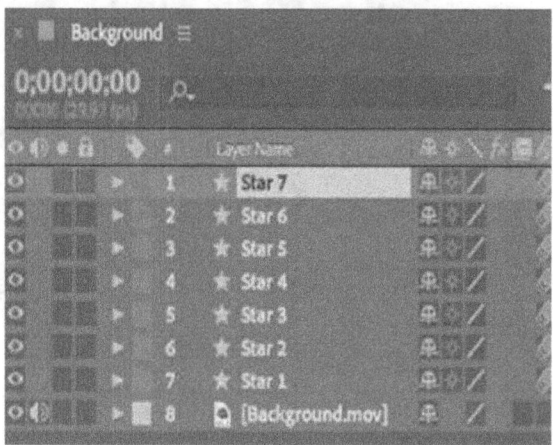

5. Next, select the Selection tool (represented by the Selection tool icon) in the Tools panel. Press F2 to deselect all layers in the Timeline panel.

Adjusting the position, scale, and rotation of each shape

Now it's time to adjust the position, scale, and rotation of each star shape. Since the stars you created are all overlapping, you need to customize their individual position, scale, and rotation.

1. Using the Selection tool, drag each star to a different position in the sky.

2. Start by selecting the Star 1 layer and then holding Shift, select the Star 7 layer. With all the star layers selected, press R, and then press Shift+S to access the Rotation and Scale properties for each layer.

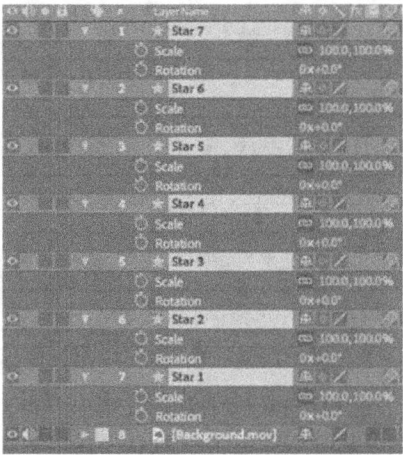

3. To deselect all layers, press F2 or click on an empty area in the Timeline panel. Then, modify the Rotation and Scale properties for each layer to introduce variation among the stars. Additionally, you can use the Selection tool to fine-tune the positions of the stars.

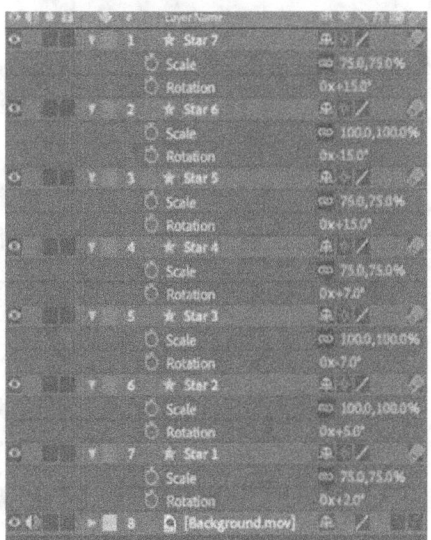

Creating Custom Shapes With the Pen Tool

The five shape tools offer a wide range of options for creating various shapes. However, the real advantage of using shape layers lies in their versatility for drawing and manipulating shapes in numerous ways.

1. To create a flowerpot's base shape, you will utilize the Pen tool. Additionally, you will animate its color to darken at the beginning of the scene and gradually lighten as the sky brightens.

2. Ensure that no layers are selected in the Timeline panel and navigate to the 1:10 timestamp.

3. Choose the Pen tool (identified by the Pen tool icon) in the Tools panel.

Within the Composition panel, click on an initial vertex and add three more vertices to draw a shape resembling the base of a flowerpot, as shown in the illustration. Finally, click on the initial vertex once again to close the shape.

When you create the first vertex, After Effects automatically adds a shape layer named "Shape Layer 1" to the Timeline panel.

4. Select "Shape Layer 1," press Enter or Return, and modify the layer's name to "Base of Flowerpot." Press Enter or Return to confirm the new name.

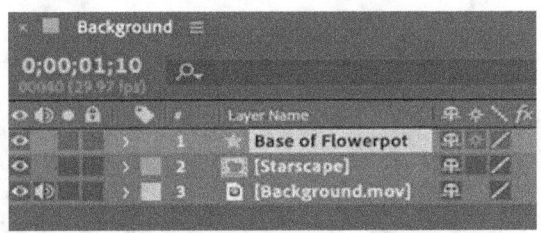

5. With the "Base of Flowerpot" layer selected, click on the Fill Color box in the Tools panel and choose a dark brown color (we used R=62, G=40, B=22).

6. Click on the word "Stroke" in the Tools panel to open the Stroke Options dialog box. Select the "None" option, and then click OK.

7. Expand the "Base of Flowerpot" layer, followed by expanding the Contents, Shape 1, and Fill 1 properties.

8. Click on the stopwatch icon next to the Color property to create an initial keyframe.

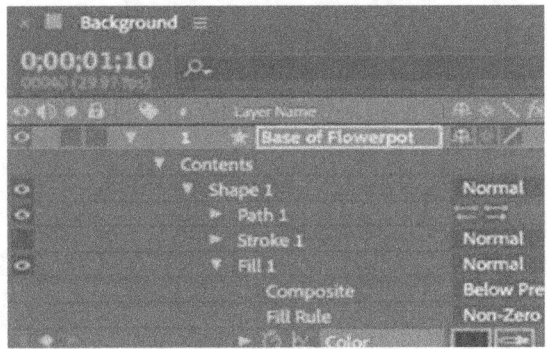

9. Navigate to the 4:01 timestamp, click on the Fill Color box, and modify the fill color to a lighter brown (we used R=153, G=102, B=59). Then click OK.

10. Hide all layer properties. Press F2 or click on an empty area in the Timeline panel to deselect all layers.

Positioning layers with snapping

Create the rim of the flowerpot and position it atop the base using the snapping feature in After Effects.

Creating a shape with rounded corners

To create the rim of the flowerpot, follow these steps:

1. Go to the 1:10 timestamp.

2. Select the Rounded Rectangle tool (identified by the Rounded Rectangle tool icon), which is hidden behind the Star tool (Star tool icon) in the Tools panel.

3. In the Composition panel, draw a shape slightly wider than the top of the flowerpot. Position the shape slightly above the base of the pot.

4. Select "Shape Layer 1," press Enter or Return, and rename the layer to "Rim of Flowerpot." Press Enter or Return to confirm the new name.

5. With the "Rim of Flowerpot" layer selected, expand the Contents, Rectangle 1, and Fill 1 properties.

6. If the rim matches the base, proceed to step 7. Otherwise, click the eyedropper next to the Color property, and then click on the base of the flowerpot in the Composition panel to sample its color.

7. Click the stopwatch icon (Stopwatch icon) next to the Color property to create an initial keyframe.

8. Go to the 4:01 timestamp and use the eyedropper tool to change the fill color to match the lighter brown in the flowerpot base.

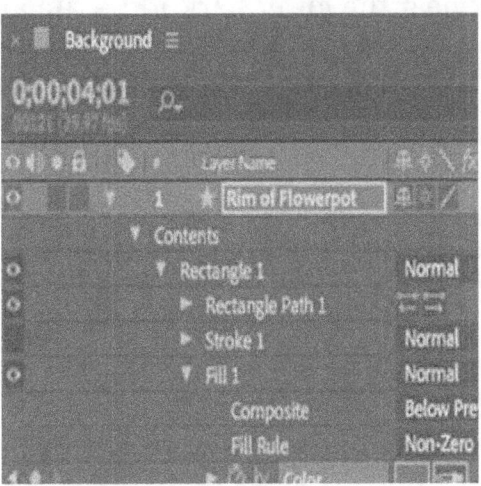

9. Hide all layer properties. Press F2 or click on an empty area in the Timeline panel to deselect all layers.

Snapping layers into position

1. If Snapping is not already selected, make sure to enable it in the options section of the Tools panel.

2. Choose the Selection tool (icon with a Selection tool) located in the Tools panel.

3. Select the "Rim of Flowerpot" layer from the Timeline panel.

   After selecting a layer in the Composition panel, After Effects will show the layer handles and anchor point. Any of these points can serve as the snapping feature for the layer.

4. Click near the lower part of the rim and drag it towards the upper edge of the "Base of Flowerpot" layer until it snaps into position. Be cautious not to drag the actual corner, as that would resize the layer.

   While dragging the layer, a box will appear around the chosen handle to indicate it as the snapping feature.

5. If necessary, use the Selection tool to adjust the size of the flowerpot's rim or base.

6. Deselect all layers and go to File > Save in order to save your work.

Animating a Shape

Shape layers offer the ability to animate various properties such as Position, Opacity, and Transform, similar to other layers. However, shape layers provide additional animation possibilities including fills, strokes, paths, and path operations.

To demonstrate this, you will create a star shape and utilize the Pucker & Bloat path operation to transform it into a flower. The animation will involve the flower falling towards a flowerpot while undergoing color changes.

Animating a path operation

Animating a path operation involves modifying a shape's path while keeping the original path intact. Path operations are editable, allowing modifications or removal at any time. Previously, you utilized the Wiggle Paths and Offset Paths path operations. Now, the focus is on applying the Pucker & Bloat path operation.

Pucker & Bloat adjusts the vertices of a path, either pulling them outward and curving the segments inward (puckering) or pulling them inward and curving the segments outward (bloating). The degree of pucker or bloat can be animated over time.

1. To begin, press the Home key or move the current-time indicator to the beginning of the time ruler.

2. Then select the Star tool, found behind the Rounded Rectangle tool in the Tools panel, and draw another star in the upper right area of the sky.

   After Effects will add a Shape Layer 1 to the Timeline panel.

3. Tap on the Fill Color box, and change the fill color to the same bright yellow you utilized for the other stars. (You can use R=215, G=234, B=23.) Then tap OK.

4. Tap on the Stroke Color box in the Tools panel, change the stroke color to a red color (you can use R=159, G=38, B=24), and then tap OK.

   After changing the stroke color, After Effects will automatically switch the stroke options from None to Solid Color.

5. To organize the layer, select the Shape Layer 1, rename it to "Falling Star," and press Enter or Return.

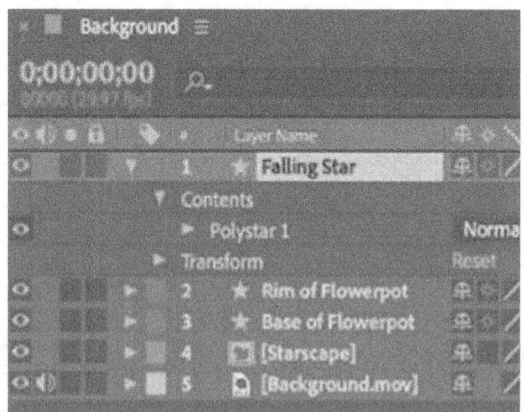

6. Then choose Pucker & Bloat from the Add pop-up menu in the Falling Star layer within the Timeline panel.

7. Expand the properties for Pucker & Bloat 1 in the Timeline panel, set the Amount to 0, and click the stopwatch icon to create an initial keyframe.

8. Proceed to the 4:01 mark and change the amount to 139.

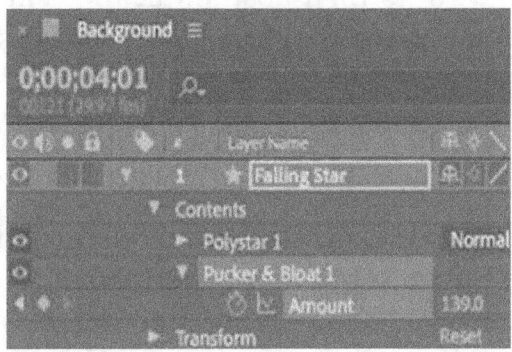

This transformation causes the star shape to become a flower, and After Effects automatically generates a keyframe.

Animating position and scale

Now, the animation will involve adjusting the position and scale of the flower.

1. Begin by pressing the Home key or moving the current-time indicator to the beginning of the time ruler.

2. Then select the Falling Star layer and reveal its Position and Scale properties by pressing P and Shift+S, respectively.

3. Click the stopwatch icon next to each property to create initial keyframes at their current values.

4. At the 4:20 mark, select the Selection tool and move the flower to its final position at the center of the screen, floating above the flowerpot between the tree and the house. To ensure accurate placement, you may need to disable Snapping in the Tools panel. At this point, the flower has transformed but hasn't changed size.

5. Return to the 4:01 mark, and increase the Scale value so that the flower becomes approximately the width of the flowerpot. The specific value depends on the original star's size and the flowerpot's width.

6. Press the spacebar to preview the animation. The flower will fall and transform, but the trajectory is currently straight.

7. To create a slight arc, go to the 2:20 mark and adjust the star's position upwards, resulting in a gentler arc for its path.

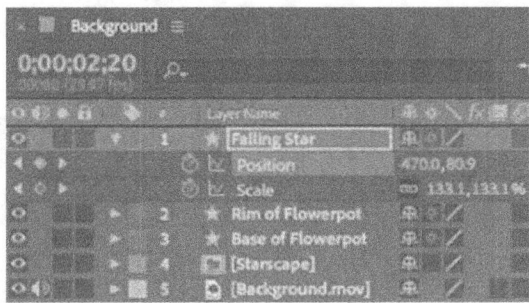

8. Preview the star's path by pressing the spacebar, and stop playback by pressing the spacebar again. If desired, you can further modify the path by adding Position keyframes at different points along the time ruler.

9. Hide the properties for the Falling Star layer.

Animating fill color

At present, the star retains its yellow color with a red stroke even after transforming into a flower. To address this, you will animate the fill color to make the final flower appear red.

1. To begin, press the Home key or move the current-time indicator to the beginning of the time ruler.

2. Expand the Falling Star layer and further expand the Contents, Polystar 1, and Fill 1 properties.

3. Click the stopwatch icon next to the Color property to create an initial keyframe.

4. Proceed to the 4:01 mark and change the fill color to a red shade. In our example, we used R=192, G=49, B=33.

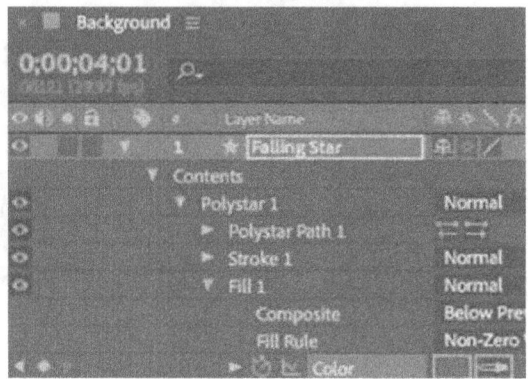

5. Hide all layer properties and ensure no layers are selected by pressing F2 or clicking on an empty area in the Timeline panel.

6. Press the spacebar to preview the animation. Press the spacebar again to stop playback. Finally, choose File > Save to save your progress so far.

www.ingramcontent.com/pod-product-compliance
Lightning Source LLC
Chambersburg PA
CBHW062352290526
45794CB00005B/2189